# Praise for
# *Roots of Redemption:*
# *You have No Right to Remain Silent*

"In this collection, Los Angeles poet Iris de Anda serves as witness to the range of travesties and tragedies resulting from the Trump Era and what came before and continues. The poet as testifier, as spy in the hole of society's conscience, as brave foot soldier who pulls the pin on the hand grenade exploding with poetic truths—Iris de Anda *¡Presente!*"

— **Ana Castillo**, *So Far From God* and *My Book of the Dead*

"Iris De Anda writes in the blood of those the unjust system has erased or silenced. She writes for the reimagined, love-filled, and peaceful world to come. I agree, Iris, let's begin again."

— **Luis J. Rodriguez**, author of *Always Running*,
*Borrowed Bones*, and *From Our Land to Our Land*

"Iris De Anda spews volcanic rage that has the potential to cauterize the bleeding heart of a severely wounded nation while roots of redemption are painfully taking hold."

— **Rubén Funkahuatl Guevara**, author of
*Confessions of a Radical Chicano Doo-Wop Singer*

"The poems in *Roots of Redemption; You Have No Right To Remain Silent* mark the spots on this colonized timeline where our young black and brown brothers and sisters have been brutalized and murdered by the police, tortured and twisted by this American nightmare…these poems are spilled sangre, a 1000 madres' sorrows and our collectivo grito over the loss of another vida that we will never see again…but make no mistake here,although these poems mark  where our familia has fallen they are NOT fallen poems, they are NOT poems of defeat but rather of resistance, rebirth, y revolution…"in the blood that was spilled the seeds were planted these are the roots of redemption taking hold" This is poesia that helps us to remember and to keep going…Iris' poems are candelas at the vigil, estrellas in el cielo."

— **Josiah Luis Alderete**, author of *Baby Axolotls & Old Pochos*

# Roots of Redemption:
# You have No Right to Remain Silent

poems by

**Iris De Anda**

FlowerSong Press
Copyright © 2022 by Iris De Anda
ISBN: 978-1-953447-12-8
Library of Congress Control Number: 2022930329

Published by FlowerSong Press
in the United States of America.
www.flowersongpress.com

Cover Art by Nico Avina aka Espacio 1839
Book Cover Design Illustration by Tenoch
Set in Adobe Garamond Pro



NOTICE: SCHOOLS AND BUSINESSES
FlowerSong Press offers copies of this book at quantity discount with bulk
purchase for educational and business use. For information, please email the
Publisher at info@flowersongpress.com.

*"A lot of people die for other people's sins."*

FUCK ICE
ACAB
LAND BACK
Justicia
NI UNA MENOS

# CONTENTS

**Immigration**
**F*#! ICE**

On Friday March 15, 2019, I was detained by the Pico Sheriff's Department in the Golden State of California. The use of excessive force resulted in 4 fractured ribs and a broken clavicle. I was denied medical attention. They did not read me my rights until Monday morning March 18, 2019. On Tuesday March 19, 2019, the sheriff purposefully made me miss my court date. I was taken to the Women's holding cell in LA County Men's Central jail. I was then taken to LA County Women's jail in Lynwood and processed for the night cause this is how the prison industrial complex makes their money. On Wednesday March 20, 2019, I was taken to court where my Public Defender had already decided my plea without even speaking to me first. I declined his first two offers because they included me staying in jail for 15 to 30 days. Finally, I plead no contest to Battery on a Peace Officer which resulted in 3 years probation and me giving up my 2nd and 4th amendment rights. I did so under duress.

**Police Brutality**

**F*#! the Police**

## When our bodies are weapons

*for Jesse Romero*


Born with original sin
In the color of our skin
Brown babies with bold becomings
Because grew up in the bad hood
Tell him to be good
Do not run
Do not walk
Do not be beautiful

Born blazing sun since first breath
He's been fighting his 14 years without knowing that one day
The bronze of his glow would fade on the asphalt
This boy from Boyle Heights
begotten of the streets where
Brown Berets still reside
Because wrong place
Wrong time
Wrong is wrong is wrong
And the blue boys
With the guns
Have wronged our rights

Before we all die
for being born brown
We will use our bodies
As billboards
Look at me
Brave despite your bondage
There is a story here
which repeats
You will beat me
until I defeat myself
On this bloody border
of badges and barrios

We are not bound by your orders
& my brothers will defy
all the blades you belt out
we are no longer
bystanders as you shoot

We are breastbone of brave mothers
who will fight for each other
The burden of your badge will collapse
on the floor covered in all the blood you spilled
Fuck the Police
our bodies are weapons
See me here unafraid
This is war

**Some Say**

*for Trayvon Martin*


Somewhere a mother
weeps blood
over daughters & sons
under the night sky
stars reflect
the fallen ones

Somehow a man
blindly walks
over history repeating
under cover of self defense
hearts break
no justice beating


Sometimes a human
seeks one truth
over generations of pain
under the gray clouds
echoes drifting
the tainted rain

Someone a boy
flys free
over unjust juries
under the flag
candles burn
the people's fury

# Mirror mirror on the wall
*(be careful lest you fall)*


I've been thinking too much lately
This always leads to conspiracy
Like ask yourself why
This is happening to humanity

Details are hidden to the naked eye
Behind symbols, numbers, & signs
Rhetoric spread across the sky
If you blink you will lose your mind

Trayvon Martin
Rings of dreams
Like the late Martin Luther King Jr.
Continued streams

Calling out racial inequality
Even from beyond
Free to be
Question authority

He just wanted to taste the rainbow
Like our LGBTQ community
Dancing outside the lines
To taste equality

He just wanted to quench his thirst Arizona
Like brothers & sisters story
Crossing borders daily
To quench memory

He was only 17
Walking from 7-11
It was not his fault
His father is Freemason

He is the sacrificed lamb
For this superficial land
He is you & me
Wondering where we stand

There is a picture
being painted here
There is more beyond
The stories we create

There is more than meets the eye
The lies the media sold
& even more behind
The stories we are told

# I can't breathe

*for Eric Garner*


I didn't write you this poem
Until his knee hit my back
As I struggled to breathe
My face on grass makes me lucky
The earth held my tears
Turned them to mud in Los Angeles
Gave me something in the form of fire

I remember hearing about you
On the news
On the social media
Your face on concrete makes you gone
The earth held your tears
Turned them to dandelions in New York
Gave us something to fight for again & again & for always

I held you in my breath
Your words echoed in my body
The man with the badge went blind with power
Because they can't see, they don't hear us
The earth holds flames and water
Turns them into volcanoes
We are too loud for this system of despair
I'm so sorry, so willing, so tired of explaining
Give us something to remember
why black and brown are not colors seen in rainbows

Even though we are the seeds
Connecting
Breath to life

## Until you are nothing
*for Michael Brown*


Here we are after all these years
Feels like the same black hole
Void deep dark cave
Where have all the young ones gone to rest?
Lights out the horizon dim
New moon reflects
our darkest hours
Humanity gone to sleep
for days & now
All around the globe the sun rays are covered by clouds
from mothers weeping because they are killing us softly
Undercover of guns
Silent system of sin
They devour the light in our eyes
To calm their fear of mud faces & ebony shine
Until you are nothing
Until you are six feet under
Until you forget you are everything
Until you surrender all dreams
Until you march to their drummer
Until you behave as the master tells you
Until you breath, stand, sit, & live white bleach
Until you no longer hear your ancestors calling because tonight after verdicts of shame
They ignore the onyx of us
because it hurts them to see smoking mirror truth rising reflections of centuries dark night
The age of genocide
Until you are under
They won't stop yet under grows fertile soil
We bloom light flowers that shine in the eyes of our black & brown sons

## Black-eyed Susans

*for Freddie Gray*

there are riots blooming in the Baltimore sun
bouquets of rage in the fists of our sons
orchids of outrage in the shouts of our moms
daisies of distress in the songs of our daughters
empty fields in the house of the forefathers
freedom flowers in the streets
to proclaim injustice
we do not need your permission
to protest
nor the barrel of your gun on our chest
to let the world know we exist
this is the ground being set on fire
for the soil was infertile and the weeds were rising
in the blood that was spilled
the seeds were planted
these are the roots of redemption taking hold
these are the shoots
reincarnated as leaves of gold
this is your American spring
this is the people uprising

## America

*the beautiful*


Does she make you rise
fall to your knees
or keep you up at night?
beautiful
Glitter in her eyes
shades of paper green
& a torch of flaming light

A-M-E-R-I-C-A

All the globe seeks your New York skyline
fashioned by rivers & corporate highs
that shine so brilliantly at sunset

Mesmerizing tales of your beauty
ring in the distance
confusing boys & girls the world over

A-M-E-R-I-C-A

I have known you all my life
nestled in the skirts of your capitalism
since my very first breath

Gasping for air amidst your consumerism
sparkles & crowns never my cup of tea
unlike you oh lady of bought up liberty

A-M-E-R-I-C-A

Sing me a better tomorrow
over too many Purple Hearts
only peace remains

Majestic fields & people's pain
unfold before you now creating
a different image of beauty & change

## Say HER name

*for Sandra Bland*


my sisters have strewn their bodies across the pavement
breath taken under moonlight
lament the way her skin blends into the night
you will forget her
the way she moved across daylight
a Queen shining from the inside

*say her name*


repeat her memory until it becomes the echo of her laughter
ignite the candles to remember our fallen daughters
pursed lips and clenched fists hold onto her
keep her safe in the ever after
for those will come who question her character
the reasons why it was and is ok to silence her

*say her name*


black women's lives matter
this american night is too dark to swallow
it is the colliding of history and those who quit listening to the master
sing her songs of freedom
she was humming the chants since birth
now we must shout until we are heard

*say her name*

Sandra Bland
Mya Hall
Tanisha Anderson
Rekia Boyd
Miriam Carey
Michelle Cusseaux
Shelly Frey

Kayla Moore
Alexia Christian
Meagan Hockaday
Breonna Taylor

*say her name*
*say her name*
*say her name*

## #bringbackourgirls

ruby rage shouts escape
as our young girls disappear
there is no sleep
when night falls without them near
days and days and days have passed
can you remember their bright eyed brilliance
forsaken flowers with petals that wither
under boots of beating  men with guns
they are killing them softly
raping them daily
silencing their spirit
every time one of them dies
can you feel it in your body
walk around so heavy
carry unseen sadness
on the bridge of our backs
they are our future failing
mountains crumbling
deserts flooding
stars extinguished after lightyears of shining
blood moon tainting the night sky
mothers wailing to the goddess
bring back our schoolgirls
bring back our daughters
they are the martyrs of this modern plague
where men get away with murdering women
while the world looks away
closed eyes to our girls plight
makes the whole world blind
you do not want to see
what you would rather neglect
because it's not your daughter, sister, or niece
you pretend to respect

can you protect morning dew from the blazing sun
the young woman from the older man
a system that teaches a girls life is worth less than his pen

there is no gentle here where our daughters cry
only rivers of pain
flowing back to the Niger
years of disdain
growing darker by the hour
bring back our sisters
bring back our feminine
bring them back
backdrop of africa
blackout of femicide
backbone of generations
backyard of transgressions
give back our girls
payback our pain
paperback our stories
comeback our angels
we are waiting
arms wide open
feet tired from running with you and for you
tongues chanting
all the ways we could pray for you
hearts broken
night and days we wait for you

bring back our girls
bring back our girls
bring back our girls

**Say HIS Name**

*For Alton Sterling & Philando Castile*


Oh say, can you see?
By the headlights
Blind in a sea of blood
Brothers shot brutal
So surreal
This repetitive reel
Of violence
Of state oppressed silence
Of ruins
Of reruns
As we watch
Wanting justice
Just once
Tell me that
Black lives matter
That a daughter
Shouldn't fear for her father
Or a lover witness
The murder
Of her other
How many times can you  say
Not one more?
No more bullets
Killing our brothers
Black as night
Bold brilliant becoming
Why the blue
Sees color
Behind the barrel
Of their brazen shot
Tell me who created
This force so full of fatality
Who will protect
us from them

Where will we run
When our tears dry
Our voices vacant from shouting
When fear forms
Around the men in uniform
When we have placed our protests
Across the land of forgotten faces
The home of empty spaces
The night falls with the fallen
And we ask for a name

## Speak back to power

Sometimes all I've ever known
Clenched in my fists
Tongue a mess
Wide eyed & discontent
Is that it is my duty
To speak back to power
Question moments
That take away a man's last breath
That incarcerate womyn in self defense
That put our youth into a percentage
Before they are old enough to
multiply and divide
all the ways the system will fail them
add and subtract
all the ways society will turn against them
because of the color of their skin
Speak back to power
bring back our movements
Black Panthers & Brown Berets
Las Adelitas de Aztlán
The Weather Underground
become the new front
for an old wound
build bridges of blossomed bones
dead students tell their tales
in the chants of the changing ones
we have never forgotten
the atrocious gunfire
that aims at our peoples pain
Speak back to power
put an end to politics
the tricks of the trade
Fall under pressure of years
that hide american nightmares
A glare of irony

Old glory rusts in ruins
Freedom fighters fuel future fires
Take the time to
Speak back to power
Speak up
Speak truth
The spoken word
Will echo, echo, echo
Good and bad
Powered and subdued
Into the end of all things

## Dreaming

*for Breonna Taylor*


A brave woman dies
While counting sheep fall asleep
To the men in blue

## Breath of Fire

*for George Floyd*


Inhale the first time
Exhale the last time
Count the time
eight minutes
forty six seconds
life
weight
anchor
    black man
blue uniform
witness
lies
camera
lies
Movement
struggle
fire
people
world
chants
om
here
now
George Floyd dreams
Minneapolis 2020
butterfly effect
crying, shouting, fighting
moving, rising, flying

# even whispers can mean war

even silence can mean death
even smiles across the wrong skin
can mean other things to other people
even now after all this politically correct
the sound of your voice
can release the bullets of a firing squad
the echo of your words
heard in the smallest of towns
can ignite unearthed rebellion
the deep inhale and exhale of your breath
the moment between us and them
even shouts can mean so little
when the disappearances say so much
so we must not let them bring your chants
to a stand still
even whispers can mean war
even secrets can mean friends
even sign language can resurrect the fallen
give them wings with whistled prayers
give them life in the dreamseeds of a poet
even too much talk and not enough action
can mean that the person talking has nowhere to go
will not let you advance too
hold you still with slithering tongue
until quicksand commands your next step to nowhere
even wind can mean rebellion
listen to the chant carried by the robins
even hope can mean resistance
even closed eyes see the truth behind lies
even songs can mean morning
our mourning dispersed across the sky
as we hear
turn volume up
rise up
stand up

don't ever give up
even whispers can mean more than this
frequency of the dispossessed
marginal offerings from those who said
too much
too fast
too soon
ignite reason with raw rage
underneath the ribcage
an acapella grace
hums notes from past composers
each one reciting symphony of creation
spinning life and death on record vinyl
smooth jazz for the soul
after decades of loud noise
which leads to nothingness
even whispers can mean war
even war can mean open hearts
ready to love again
listen again
begin again

## 4/22/2020

*For Vanessa Guillen*


Master numbers behind
Master plan
undercover of FORT HOOD
Twenty year old
Mexican American found
On the grounds of secrecy
    under investigation
Brings down a nation's lies
Moonlight exposes the threat of military life
Direct aim at our communities
To join the killing machine
Give up rights for so called democracy
Bribed in plain sight
Recognize the impunity of stacked generals
Holding false stars and stripes
Digress from freedom
When our daughters
Learn to fight then die
Dead girls tell no tell tales
Count
5 homicides
7 suicides
8 accidents
2 illnesses
5 deaths
When know one knows why
Still her mother doesn't know why
So we put this system under scrutiny
And demand an apology which will never materialize
But we are the daughters of struggle
The daughters of pain
The daughters born of rain and thunder
And we will get our answer fortified
Under full moon and fire

We are she reborn again and again
There is no going back
This is her scorn
And we the ones that will make it so

## Freedom

*for Ashraf Fayadh*


Instructions within *
Let us not be afraid to listen
Words are our strongest medicine
Inside of us
The wisdom of ancients
In our tongues
A new horizon
In our lips
Whispers of warriors
How do you quiet
The fire of those
Who awakens the masses?
Take away their pen
& their right to publish
Incarcerate the person
But never the prophet
The words will flow on regardless
Let us
Choose love lovers
Choose books over guns
Choose letters over lies
Just us juxtapositioned with historic violence
Our lungs fill up with poetic justice


*Fayadh was arrested in 2013 concerning his poetry collection Instructions Within.*
*In 2015, he was sentenced to death in connection with a collection of his poems.*
*In 2016 after an appeal he was sentenced to 8 years in jail and 800 lashes.*
*He is still in prison.*

# VII IV

I
*July 4, 2016*

United States of Us All A Mess
This here land that was Stolen
Built on Blood of Ancestors
So we dream up false idols
Drink away our troubles
All waving a flag of fallen stars


II
*July 4, 2017*

Number 45
is
not my President
is
Racist
is
another white man
in
the White House
is
a threat to our freedom


III
*July 4, 2018*

Dressed in weeping cages
Lady Liberty isn't free
As the echoes of children
Tell us the tale of this AmeriKKKa
Once the land of the promise
We digress to the truth of this eve
Flags of red white and stolen land

Make us blue
Make us accomplices or traitors
Make us the home of ancestors blood
They have denied our humanity
In stages, as we recount the ways
Uncle Sam betrayed himself
Under a constitution that is being stripped before our eyes & ears & hands &
mouths
Wake up as hawk feathers pierce our dreams*
Foretelling the prophecies of old
As you see fireworks in the night sky
Understand that bombs are not bridges &
People are not property &
Our hearts are not cages &
Our children are not collateral &
All that you sow, you will reap
On this soil of sorrow & sweat
For the next seven generations
We say enough is enough
We are blooming in the desert of this dying democracy
We are the rage and the rose
We are the flame and the footsteps
We are the witness and the water
Flowing forward with fists full of love

*dreams as spoken about by Dr. Martin Luther King, Jr.

IV
*July 4, 2019*

Conceived by two foreign birds
Born in a nest of stars & stripes
My tongue sings at dawn over borders
My eyes pierce the dusk of this nation
Count the 9 numbers of citizen stamped across my chest
Strip me of this flags shame
Make me human
Make me mujer
Make me mother
Tie me to the cages where the children cry
So they may pluck the eagles wings one by one

Then make a dreamcatcher for their stay
In the nightmare of america the fraud
In the memory of their dead at the river
In the hopes that fireworks are an SOS to the world
Come now
Come look
Come save us


V
*July 4, 2020*

The fireworks implode
Spiderwebs catch them by a thread
Deciphering Dreamtime & Nightmares
Of black and brown blood
Make us bleed awake
Dripping genocide
In a Cul De Sac
Remember me when I'm dead
Veins exploding across your television set
Lock us up
Make us kneel
Make us bow
Spoiled brats light the stage
To a system of regrets
This is not a familiar set
When you close your eyes
To Stolen lands
Territory of the ancients
Manifests into this here & now
This creation of lament
2020 vision is not what it seems
Realize it was only a livestream
Press record
Press play
Stay inside the matrix for another day
Don't remember why you came
Starseeds lifting up your name
Into black holes and unknown galaxies
Spirals of future memory
Quarantine is not your fate

You came to recreate
This story takes place
Inside your heart
So dream yourself awake
And fuck those who disengage
Fuck the United States of A

## 10-4

Wakes up
Lace up
Black boots
Purple & Blue Baton
Packs bullets for breakfast
Lines pockets with Miranda RIGHTs
Will never turn LEFT
Especially when following orders
Starts the day slow
Drawls out the gun with reflex
When dark skin comes to sight
Slangs power on their belt while
A hookem & bookem anthem
Plays berries & cherries to the masses
Only wears a body cam when it doesn't clash
With the victim's blood or rights
Masks up the bros bill of secrets
Cause this is the gang gang
The new hood mafia
The wannabe sheriffs in town
The red apple of the machine
One a day kills our children at play
Leaves us to grieve
While nobody pays justice to society
There is no black only white
There are no good cops
Only bad seeds

# Immigration

F*#! ICE

## Untitled

I dream in English
but when I dream
I pray in Spanish
this must be the language
of my corazón

**Freedom**

*Hola Niñxs,*


*Duerme tranquilo mi niño*
*Yo manaña espero*
*Yo nunca te olvido*
*Yo nunca te olvido*


Te quiero mucho
Tu no me conoces pero todas las noches
Yo prendo una vela por ti
Esperando que te regresen a tu mami


*Duerme tranquilo mi niño*
*Yo manaña espero*
*Yo nunca te olvido*
*Yo nunca te olvido*

# Coyote Dreams

*Hay quienes te dicen Radical*
*yo hiciera lo mismo*
*todos somos igual*
*Ya Basta criticismo*

this is for
some of the people
I love the most

Hunger Strike
Front Lines
Direct Action
Fight for Rights
Dream 9 to Dream 30 to Dream Everyone

this is for
some of the people
I love the most

The day I risked myself
to cross over a loved one

No time to think
about consequence
Only reuniting a family
focused outcome

In the moment
no more heartbreak
Only a dream
of coming home

this is for
some of the people
I love the most

When the dreamers
took things into their own hands

It is not up to us
to make demands
They cannot wait
for someone else to take a stand

It is not about us
It is about them
Only they know
the circumstance

this is for
some of the people
I love the most

My parents set foot here
without proper papers
My ex husband was brought here
without proof of residence

My heart does not ask
for their status
Love is not bound
by borders

We are not here
to judge others

this is for
some of the people
I love the most

Home is where the heart is
Heart is with our family
Family is what makes this life
Life is why we dream
Dreams is where the change comes

## La Bestia / The Beast

*"The journey towards you Lord, is life. To
set off, is to die a little. To arrive is never
to arrive, until one is at rest with you. You,
Lord, experienced migration. You brought
it upon all men who know what it is to
live; who seek safe passage to the gates
of heaven. You yourself became a
migrant from heaven to earth."*

metallic snake of rust and tears
weaving your way through the Sierra Madre
carrying those who carry hope
leaving candles lit in their passing
asking for safe passage to el norte
land of green dollar dreams

el tren de la muerte
the train of death
hundreds of thousands of hands
reached towards your hot sun
son of the road so travelled
there are stories about your story
slivering steel tracks on midnight stations
the migrants life to reach their haven
another day
another dream

el tren de los desconocidos
the train of the unknown
perilous journey to the other side of the wall
across barbed wires of illusion
delusion of constructed reality
all are born free
earth is boundless territory
so our hermanos run onto railroads
as our hermanas drift to new destinos

quetzalcoatl underground
winding your wheels through pachamama
unraveling esperanza in empty fields
lucid movements of unspoken songs
traveling upward toward light
maravilla echoes in gringo
el tren de mil cuatrociento cincuenta millas
the train of 1450 miles
opening its mouth daily
devouring the youth of third world
never enough blood spilled
on this holy migrant trail
the rivers are turning to wine
sacrifice of mothers offspring
all hungry
all thirsty

el tren del mañana
the train of tomorrow
escaping small town poverty
send the familia money
rewrite the story
step into the glory of miracles
when one of these travelers
arrives en el otro lado
arrives naked but alive

## Jamás se Olvida / Never Forgotten

*"Por qué el color de la sangre jamas se olvida*
*Los masacrados serán vengados*
*Vestidos de verde olivo*
*Políticamente vivos*
*No has muerto, no has muerto, no has muerto camarada*
*Tu muerte, tu muerte, tu muerte será vengada*
*¿Y quien la vengara?*
*El pueblo organizado*
*¿Y como?*
*Luchando, pues lucha, lucha, lucha*
*No dejes de luchar*
*Por un gobierno obrero campesino y popular"****

Remembering your life
as if you were still here
as if you never left our family
as if you will always remain

Remembering your death
as if you weren't one of many
as if you kissed that tragic end
as if you transcended pain

Remember
I will always
Remember

Remembering your ideals
as if you are still near
as if you inspire my path
as if you sacrificed for our future

Remembering your love
as if you can still embrace
as if you visit me in dreams
as if you whisper truths in our sleep

Remember
I will always
Remember

Every fallen angel
fallen brother/sister
fallen hero
fallen story

Remembering you are me
I AM you
we are they
& you are here still
always
hearts beating
hearts beating
hearts beating

***canto del pueblo


**Fernando Franco Delgado**
**Juan Gonzalez del Castillo**
**Natalia Velasquez**
**Soren Ulises Aviles Angeles**

# Tú

Tú que hoy vuelas
con el amanecer
despiertas de colores
con mariposas
fragrancias de Cempasuchil

Tú eres heroe del Castillo
con palabras que
se quedan en mi memoria
azul como el mar
que te lleva a descansar

Tú existes en mi lucha
con aliento dulce
murmuras de noche
con el viento
lluvia de Estrellas

Tú vives para siempre
con musica fuerte
bailando zapateado
con la Catrina
cerca del cielo

Tú te fuistes muy pronto
con palabras por decir
horizontes que ver
con parte de mi
clavada en tu Corazón

Tú regresas cada año
con velas y tequila
vestido de fiesta
con cuentos de mañana
risas como Rey

Tú atraviesas el tiempo
con sueños bordados
cruzas fronteras
con espíritu brillante
reflejas la Luna

Tú y Tú y Tú
Siempre aquí
Siempre presente
Siempre Tú
adentro de mi

## Rojo Amanecer

*"No somos todos señores,*
*nos faltan 43*

*Este gobierno corrupto señores,*
*nos quiere desaparecer*

*El Pueblo camina junto*
*queremos al Mundo despertar*

*Desde La Frontera hasta Chiapas señores*
*la lucha contra el poder"****

Tapame los ojos
Que ya no puedo ver
El duelo de mi país
Otro rojo amanecer
El gobierno es maestro de la oscuridad
Los estudiantes ejercen la luz
Es por eso que los de arriba
Dan órdenes para apagar
El fuego del pueblo
Pues les ilumina
Su corrupcion
Pero les falla su matanza
Porque por cada vela que apagan
Se encienden 43 mas y mas y mas
Cuarenta y tres semillas de luz digna rabia
Se estremece el mundo entero
La humanidad está de luto
Y los 43 viven en su llanto
No dejes que te llenen de miedo
La justicia es tu arma
Y el sol tu aliento
Porque otro rojo amanecer
No podemos aguantar
Sigue luchando
Mi gente presente

La luz es de quien la enciende
Tu voz es un altar
Recordamos a los caídos
Los levantamos en nuestro gritar
Ya basta Ayotzinapa
Tu sembraste un campo de ideas
Ahora la cosecha despierta

Ombligo de México nace tu revancha

El gobierno no se queda impune
Porque el pueblo se levanta
Levantate hermano
Levantate ya
Tus compañeros te apoyan
Desde el desierto y la montaña
Cruzamos fronteras
Unimos las manos
Tu duelo es el mio
Y tu noche la mía
Marchamos con luz de dia
Exigimos justicia


*** *canto del pueblo*

Felipe Arnulfo Rosa, Benjamín Ascencio Bautista, Israel Caballero Sánchez, Abel García Hernández, Emiliano Alen Gaspar de la Cruz, Dorian González Parral, Jorge Luis González Parral, Magdaleno Rubén Lauro Villegas, José Luis Luna Torres, Mauricio Ortega Valerio, Jesús Jovany Rodríguez Tlatempa, Abelardo Vázquez Penten, Adan Abraján de la Cruz, Christian Tomás Colón Garnica, Luis Ángel Francisco Arzola, Carlos Lorenzo Hernández Muñoz, Israel Jacinto Lugardo, Julio César López Patolzin, José Ángel Navarrete González, Marcial Pablo Baranda, Miguel Ángel Mendoza Zacarías, Alexander Mora Venancio, Bernardo Flores Alcaraz, Luis Ángel Abarca Carrillo, Jorge Álvarez Nava, José Ángel Campos Cantor, Jorge Aníbal Cruz Mendoza, Giovanni Galindes Guerrero, Jhosivani Guerrero de la Cruz, Cutberto Ortiz Ramos, Everardo Rodríguez Bello, Chistian Alfonso Rodríguez Telumbre, Martín Getsemany Sánchez García, Jonás Trujillo González, José Eduardo Bartolo Tlatempa, Leonel Castro Abarca, Miguel Ángel Hernández Martínez, Carlos Iván Ramírez Villarreal, Jorge Antonio Tizapa Legideño, Antonio Santana Maestro, Marco Antonio Gómez Molina, César Manuel González Hernández y Saúl Bruno García

## Escuelitas

Cuando llegaron los Zapatistas
Al escenario mundial
Yo sentí respirar más profundo
apareci despertar de un sueño
Largo y oscuro
El sol brillaba más claro
Mi corazón se exaltó
Y sentí danzar en ritmo
De tambores
Lejanos pero mios

Inspirada por mis compañeros
Me cubri mi cara
Solo revelando mis ojos
Cafe caoba
Que reflejaban
Una mañana sin dueño

Clame palabras
Que nadaban en mi ser
Y entendí que no estaba solo
Que la revolución
No comprada
Si no es un latido
Que crece cada vez
Que nace un rebelde
Como tu
Como yo
Como ellos

Hermanos y Hermanas
De la tierra que toca el cielo
Respirar profundo
Ahora si
La humanidad
Escoje su destino

## El Grito

Fuerte y con valor
Cuántos hombres y mujeres
Derraman sangre
Por su patria
Parece fácil, lindo y heroico
En memoria
Como cosa de cada dia
Como capullo y mariposa
Como caracol y tortuga
En camino lento
Avanza siempre por el escudo
De la noche
Paciente y con rabia
Los pueblos se levantan
sonando libre
Por su tierra
En recuerdos nos perdemos
Encontramos y crecemos
Cómo lluvias que alimentan la vida
Como semilla y árbol
Crece la resistencia
Como flor y palabra
Cuentan la historia
Presente y con ganas
Reunimos la lucha
Honesta y verdadera
Para todos los que escuchan


*Ya Basta!*
*Si Se Puede!*
*Que Viva*
*Que Viva*
*Que Viva!*

## Manos a la Obra

Muchas manos
Poco trabajo
Los de arriba más arriba
Y nosotros abajo
La ley del obrero
Trabajar para comer
Comer para trabajar
Salir a buscar jale
Cuando el sol sale
La fortaleza de nuestros abuelos
Presente cada momento
Vivir vida digna
Luchar por el pueblo
La circunstancia hace al hombre
Y este sistema a nosotros
Hay que seguir con honra
Hasta lograr más que sobre vivencia
La luz es de los que la reflejan
Juntos hermanos crecemos
Valientes y con esperanza
Por un mejor mañana

# Jornalero

Tu fuerza como el sol
Tus manos alimentan la vida
Tu dedicación alienta el dia
Tu sudor derrama memoria
Tu buscas hasta encontrar
Tu sigues sin descansar
Tu trabajo o muchos inspira
Tu sueñas con mucha alegría
Tu camino lleno de lucha
Tus plegarias todos escuchan
Tu dia a dia bajo el calor
Tu presencia llena de valor
Tu ganas el respeto
Tu hombre jornalero

## La Pocha de la Libertad

Te pareces a la statue de liberty
asi bien pretty
con tus flores verdes
banderas picadas
y estrellas caídas

Holding patriotic
at the tip of your tongue
head held high
emotions a mess
because you love everyone
you set your eyes on

Night sky
in the wind of your hair
boots grounded deep
swift sign language
between strangers
you know better than me

Cross my heart
& hope to live
somewhere between
the land of dreams
& the tierra of mañana

Ay, querida luna
que atraviesas fronteras
tu reflejas mi corazón
de alas y promesas
en un lugar
que no existe

Pocholandia dreams
linguistic streams

to nowhere
to now here
to the summer
of our discontent


*dedicated to Jose Montoya el maestro who reminds us our stories still need to be told*

**mamá**



querida madre
gracias infinitas
por darme la vida

you who wake early
to help me RISE
you who sleep late
to watch me DREAM

you who are my everything
from first breath to last
you hope for my future
& stood by my past

querida madre
sin ti no soy yo
te amo

# PAPÁ

This is for my father
& his father
& the fathers before them
for their courage
to continue the family line
Even thru the hard times

Sitting in this chair
there are sounds
like orchestra music
deep breaths
& life seeking alternatives
there are screens
holding images of universes
lines & numbers creating balances
there are feelings
in the air
of high hopes & despair
I choose the first
with hands in prayer
I offer up these words
like smoke signals
to the creator
bless the hands
of all who work here
dedicate their lives
to caring for others
day shifts
night shifts
all adrift
today is questionable
what brought you here?
loss of time
loss of memory
delusion lies

in the eyes
of medicine

May the results
be positive
believe in miracles
we are survivors
ancestors visit
fill the waiting room
there is no hesitation
just beings in bloom
that new health
finds its way
to your body
find new life
breathing light
amidst the ordinary
second chances
few & far between
so give thanks today for living

## siStars

here we are
after years
crossing borders
wings & wire
monarch butterfly
flutter over under
forest redwood
storm cloud
arid desert
spring dahlia
carrying hope on chest
dreams in corazon
i am dreaming
this here now
this you I
this us them
we are all together
there was no time
no space
no borders
only jade spiral
obsidian death
coral life
growing blooming
touching creating
sleeping awakening
sighs
luz consciousness
la mujer
rises morning sun
luz roja
amarilla naranja
refleja reflects
a mirror
deep waves

profundo azul
everywhere floating
lotus crying
daughter of beating
pain buried
dark womb
crystals surface
daughter of beating
mother earth drums
corazon dreams
mud feet
daughter of beating
clay dance
bruja guerrera
yourself
herself
sistars

# Lingua Franca

I have no language
to tell stories
forgotten tapestry
torn maps

I have no language
but my body moves
across borders
forbidden dance

I have no language
spilling bloodlines
marked pen on paper
draw memory

I have no language
as it was taken
500 years ago
by blade in secrecy

I have no language
heritage lost
interwoven past
ghostwriter

I have no language
the luggage of continents
buried my soul
across mountains

I have no language
disguised as song
the verses inside my head
are hummingbirds flight

I have no language
but the sun speaks
the moon murmurs
for me days and nights

I have no language
but energy rises
spin web of words
in the iris of my eye

I have no language
that is not mine
universal tongue
intertwines inside

I have no language
yet spit fire
commune with community
silence is everything

I have no language
but language has me
as I transverse poetic highway
meet midnights muse

I have no language
which does not penetrate
for every sound
my lover listening

I have no language
but you have them all spoken
written on every inch of your palm
when our hands touch my palm speaks

# Glow Up

our skin sun kissed at birth
some keep reaching for el sol
look under rocks & white hoods for answers
their ancestors forgot to keep
our abuelas tucked amulets into our braids
formed alliances with the trees
to carry messages thru their roots to find us
whispered pachamama lullabies into our veins
made our mamas strong with traditions and cuentos

our gente is pure gold reflecting el sol
place us anywhere in the world and we shine sunrise
working where no one else wants to
stretching fingertips into fields and factories of capitalism
placing one foot in front of the other
feeling blessed in this bruised world
some of them mistake our brilliance for brutality
take our lives under the veil of democracy
while spitting racist fumes of self hate
our abuelos raised us with a steady hand
placed dirt under our fingernails so we would always have soil to plant gardens
strummed guitar strings into our hair to dance with the people around us
made our Fathers soft with dreams and drive

our gente is the minerals that reflect life
place us in cages  and we become songbirds of resilience
bringing light to dark histories
awakening the masses to the massacre of freedom
screaming soft cries in front of a wailing wall
feeling betrayed by el norte
the north star blinded the people, numbed the people, herded the people
the sun woke up the people, healed the people, freed the people
our nanas and tatas encoded stars and maps into our eyes to guide us
thru this dark age in the United States of America
you can glow up whenever you want to

## Genocide

gather on this day of genocide
round a table of tears
mask the memories
stones and feather amulets
flesh and bone altars our alibi
our elders come home from graves
mark your calendars
season of the archer aims at Chiron's wound
dissolves in a ceremony of muddy stars
when giving is taking
blindfolds imbued with wine
ask for this nations reparations
the cage is the new plymouth rock
ice the new conquistador
our children the next seven generations
our silence complacency
drumbeats a foundation of resistance
exists in us
protest this pilgrim
split the family system
cause we risin' in the skies
taking over this land once again
it has been prophesied
the seven sistars are present
fate wove them into our timeline
witness pachamama lift us
mark your place in this cycle of life
decide to take back what is our cosmic birthright

# About the Author

Iris De Anda a Guanaca Tapatia poet, speaker & musician who has been featured with KPFK & KPFA Pacifica Radio, organized with Academy of American Poets, performed at Los Angeles Latino Book Festival, Feria del Libro Tijuana, Mexico, Casa de las Américas in Havana, Cuba and is named one of Today's Revolutionary Women of Color. Author of *Codeswitch: Fires from Mi Corazon*.

# Acknowledgements

Tlazocamati Creator.Ometeotl.Om.Namaste.Sat Nam.
All is One.
I AM grateful to everyone on my path.
I give thanks to my Abuelas & Abuelos for instilling the resilience of generations
in my braids.
Mi familia. Mi comunidad. Mis amigx.
***

Reclaim and Rebuild our Communities - RROC
Eastside Cafe - Los Angeles, 90032
Mujeres de Maiz
EnCholadas - Rebecca Gonzales & Xitlalic Guijosa Osuna
Brujas - Tara Evonne Trudell & Jeanette Iskat
Las Lunas Locas - {you} know who {you} are
Tierra de la Culebra - Soraya Medina, Raymond Grate, Joy Dueñez, & David Lasky
Las Cruxes & Vision
Falcon
Luminaries - Josh Duron & Joy Anderson
Mushroom Medicine Warrior  & Spirit SiStar - Diana Herrera
My Best Friend  & Mirror, Forever & Always in All Ways  - Monica Oregon
***

Art work by Nico Avina aka Espacio 1839
Book Cover Design Illustration by Tenoch

For all the poets who show up as strangers this is for {you} too.

FUCK ICE
ACAB
LAND BACK
Justicia
NI UNA MENOS

"I love America more than any other country in this world, and, exactly for this reason, I insist on the right to criticize her perpetually."

— James Baldwin

www.ingramcontent.com/pod-product-compliance
Lightning Source LLC
Chambersburg PA
CBHW040234170726
48295CB00014B/916

9 781953 447128